www.bolerobird.ca

Other Books From Bolero Bird

Lo-Fi - Michael Whone (2022)

Poor, Pretty Creature - Ciara Selene (2020)

River Van Style Review vol. 1: Gross Restore (2019)

There Is A Light That Never Goes Out - Michael Whone (2018)

Winter Lyric - Michael Whone (2017)

LITTLE BIT DIE

Bolero Bird edition 2023
Copyright © 2023 Jason Emde
All Rights Reserved

Library and Archives of Canada
Emde, Jason
little bit die / Jason Emde
Bolero Bird 1st Edition
ISBN: 978-1-7753300-7-3
Book Design by River Van Style

www.bolerobird.ca

for
Stanley Czerwonka
1971-2013

LITTLE BIT DIE

vernon

stranger

*I'd wander its cosmopolitan winter streets in a trance, thinking of my own future
and imagining all of us doing great things and finding happiness in different way*
— John Lent, "Matins 16, February 7, 2016"

Vernon a childhood goontown of dissimilar yelling kids
vastly different from Gifu now as my own kids grow up, Gifu
with its waves of school uniforms & uniform hair &
everybody using the exact same words & Gifu
loudspeakers telling them all to go home at 5 P.M.
Vernon had stranger swarms, we skylarked
from dark to dark with neighbourhood gangs, half-Chinese
brothers, white kids, weird religious kids, anybody,
in the snow or forest fire afternoons, building
jumps in the street for our banana-seat bikes & clambering
in the dusk over everything. Anybody. It's true.
Those we then called East Indians, the family
down the street, satiny flash of a sari in a split-level doorway.
Or those we then called Indians, the First Nations kids,
some scary, one time one angry boy
shouting in the playground, yelling
at the *white bitches*, meaning all of us, tough in those jeans,
his resentment radiant—or a girl
named Julie, I kissed her at the dance, went once to her
house on the reservation, vast mysterious area outside
of town—or Tommy, oddball Indigenous kid
down the block who named his cat *Stranger*. Loads
of Ukrainians, Yablonskis, Yakimovitches, rumours of Russian Gangs
later, & the Germans across the street, old & gruff, I accidentally
shot an arrow onto their roof. Asians, Vietnamese,
those two no-English brothers so ropey with muscles & feral
eyes nobody'd fight them, or Lan I liked,
held her hand in the Towne Theatre watching *2010*.
Gary American & Jewish, Geoff adopted, Stan Polish,
Jed Russian, me German-English, & Stewart rich.
Delicate essential exchange students from Spain, South Africa,
Sweden, Finland, New Zealand, Zimbabwe. Who else?
Magnet-throwers of the lightning storm, heroes
of the roller rink, victims of the corner store. Also poor
kids, botched kids, the kid who ate
a dog turd at the bus stop, bike-stealers, bullies,
liars, the frothing gang that stomped

Jed in the Surplus Herbies parking lot,
the sullen kid who slugged Gary for no reason at the
mall, various small-town psychopaths,
that one family with the Doberman & the dope,
jerks of many kinds. I could be a jerk too.
The manners & textures of the times, the days, Vernon days,
innumerous the colours & shapes, weird to think of it now, it was only after all
backwards backwater shitkick Vernon, myriad distinct. Everything there.
And everything was mostly ok though we had our vile & shameful
moments I guess, jokes, unexamined hang-ups, snickering principles,
secrets in the air, densities, sidewalk punch-ups. Nobody
was gay though, nobody at all, though they probably are now, can't say,
haven't been a kid in Vernon for a long time.

through the hedge & over the fence

frost giants cranked up to ten winding the town into winter   all this thin cold
black rocks in dirty snow   & the iron streets

our long oikophobic walks   down 27th Street   past all these churches
in the Canadian dark
determined to dismiss the town   fill the quiet with our talk   & walk it down
past the mall   past Swan Lake   to the icebound outskirts
& the sign that says *out*

we just gotta get outta here Stan   stop fucking around & get right the fuck out
I'm not talking about a hitchhike to Banff   (over the mountains: snowpink of a fire
or the strip club in Kelowna   or roaming Robson & Granville
on the rainy ragged edge of the continent
nothing like that

let's reject the long drive back from Kootenays
or coast   gravel-dark of driveway   & holidays done
let's reject together this ghost-less town
reject fussing with our folks
reject no kisses landing, no kisses launched
reject mowing the lawn   shoveling the driveway
let's dig the diamond suitcases out from under the stairs   break our lives in half
sling our hooks   & leave Vernon flat
break free from our long strings of crushes & handjobs   just hell be damned
& look out
go elsewhere   find some hubbub   some tumult   big noise
jump from the top of a Guangzhou minaret   jump off Fuji
wander out of the codes here   & into humid confusion   raucous omnishamble
big city clatter   snake wine & baijiu   rooms & scenes, caves & crows
switchblades   tropical mists   riverine bars   typhoons
& Gobi Desert sand
vault over   to plunge in
& embrace the voltage of the world-pearl

let's *go*, man

kal lake

How old was I when I
first saw Kalamalka Lake?
I guess five. Saw it last six
years ago when I went back to see
Stan's grave & cash
the check from his estate.

Dad's house:
walk five minutes down Kickwillie Loop
& there you are. Ten minutes more
to Kal Beach. Conglomerate
summer smells: coconut suntan
oil, hot sand, french fry grease.

Sunday afternoons splashing
in the chilly shallows with
my brother & sister,
Dad reading the paper
under a tree
after church.

Or the great state of high
& released, screaming with laughter
on Pumphouse Beach
with Stan & Max & Tom
the night of my book launch
the summer my mother died.

The famous sinking greens of the lake
a function of limestone crystals
reflecting the sunlight
at particular temperatures.
Emerald shiftings round
the tip of Rattlesnake Point.

Can't remember now exactly why
I was so eager to leave it,
to leave. The lake & its town.
How old was I then? Twenty-four.
More than twice that age now
& hurt in the heart away.

things to do around vernon
    after Gary Snyder

Jump over the place where the creek gets narrow
Feast on the noise of the Northern lights, feast on the hum of the orchard
Dodge purely imaginary downtown gangs of thugs & goons
Enjoy famous agrestic gingham settler history at famous O'Keefe Ranch
Wash giant pots all summer long in minimum wage cadet camp kitchen
Scrape two dozen ticks off your legs
Walk four kilometres into town to bum one cigarette
Get first hickey at summer camp from a girl from Edmonton
    distributing them freely to whomsoever come who may
Climb up onto Main Street rooftop talk about girls with Stan
Get punched out at the library
All them apples, all them peaches
Try to impress Tiffany P. with your *Hey Jude* watch
Fall out of the tree, fall off the fence, fall out the window with
    plum blossoms in your hair
Feel up Leslie K. backstage, in the graveyard, on Xmas couch, in
    Stewart's room, everywhere you can
Set Stewart's house on fire by accident with flaming paper airplane
Gladiator crabapple, great blue heron, Douglas maple, cedar
    waxwing, ponderosa pine, tundra swan, chokecherry, rain-beetle
Buy *On the Road* at Bookland & upgrade all your heroes & plans
Scribble first inept poems in first secret notebooks
Apply for Rotary Student Exchange ask for India Thailand Zimbabwe
Largest floral clock in western Canada

while I'm away from here

        the outer ribs protect
        the inner ribs
        bamboo or bone
            but
        Vernon busted both, busted
        whatever China had built for him
                  Better if I had never
                  gone at all
                              he said

        Polish kid from Vernon
        happy at last in China
            all the spaces awakened

            until

        altogether too gentle
            too passive
                & yielding

        Stan not seasoned enough
            or master enough
                to resist

        insufficient protection
        from cruel shocks out the mouth of
        his first & only girlfriend, words
            thrown, words
            stabbed

                I threw a glass of wine at the wall
                            he said
                    as proof of—what?
                    flaw? defect? easy target?

mother dead & father dead & finally
China fading also
            all of which
                threw his reflection into disarray,
                the pond
                broken
the return to Vernon was
            the key that locked
            him in &
            clicked him closed

crying in park & backyard

my friend crying
    in park & backyard

& you always so discreet

when you

went & died

you made

dying true

let it in

& made it real

if you can die

Maho can die

my kids

can die

Max & Patrick & Tom

can die

my kids

can die

O man Stan

that was

a truly

shitty thing

to let me

in on

like that

young together in all kinds of light

    Leave my sons & wife, fly to Vernon, stay
    in my old bedroom in Dad's house,
    admire the books & pictures:
    my friends & me in Zimbabwe, Malawi, Swaziland, Vancouver,
    Mexico, America, Paris, Poland. — Look out the window
    at my valley, my rattlesnake hills, my lake.

    Walk Highway 97 to downtown,
    walk through my memories strung all over from
    1976 on, parades, movies at the Towne,
    coffee shops of my college days, routines,
    the poolhall, Hung Phat's where Geoff worked,
    Bookland, Backstreets, places no longer where they were.

    The Kal Hotel on its corner since 1892 much
    diminished now, full of phantoms, my phantoms, gone.
    All the alcoholic evenings, yelling talk or whispering.
    Sit in there alone today hoping for connection
    beyond ego & hope, signs from anywhere, but
    it isn't like the old days & I still am. And now

        (tending towards *ours* at last)
        I veer through images flashing,
        careen 30 years of us in our days
        together in our everything
        even when we weren't & it wasn't even true.

            a lot of time, a lot of many years
            a lot of arms around each other
                (staggering with our arms,
                staggering home singing)
            a lot of arcade faces bent to laser kung-fu in Friday's
            a lot of isotropic talk
            a lot of bar carpet footfalls, glimmer dims of afternoons
                right here in our Kal
            a lot of iron Polish dark you knew & I went to see & know
            a lot of alarmingly smart with laughter & blast
                before smart went cold

a lot of stuff that never killed us
a lot of I love you & I love you still
a lot of goodbye stretching both forward & back
    & not enough, but a lot of our light

I only remember stupid stuff

    These days I only have 2
    phone numbers memorized:
    my dad's, & yours:
    545-2904

    the long spinning wait
    for the nine, for the zero
    our old black phone
    a rotary, downstairs

    calling after 10 o'clock
    on weekend mornings long ago
    before Japan for me
    & China for you

    can still see your phone
    its kitchen counter
    & the table there
    we talked across

    useless, now
    like everything else
    when I turn
    to reach you, Stan

in ghostly vernon

    Stan your ghost in Vernon always knew it there
    Your ghost shy in poolhall
            crying on Bearisto swings broken-hearted
                  screaming laughter birthday party sleepover pizza
    Your ghost in the chorus of *Take This Waltz*
            in Kal Hotel saloon afternoons
                giggling with me shitfaced in Roger's closet
                    driving back from Penticton bookstore
    Your ghost in the alley at the top of your loneliness
            anchored to the rock at the lake
                in unopened mail
                    in the struggle to the last Okanagan ditch
                      in Russian POW camp with your father
                          as the guards hunt
                              grassland wolves
    Your ghost rotating in a Polish core
    Your ghost in Ebenezer's, in Libra Adult Video
                on our long march around nighttime fall smoking first cigarettes
                on springtime main street rooftop with me
    Your ghost home from China sad
    Your ghost in 545-2904
            bald & fat
                in the sign saying *out*
                      in the copy of *On the Road* we left at your grave
    Your ghost full of excuses
    Your ghost stuck in Vernon
            Stan
haunting my vaults
even now
even from here

portrait of the pal as a revisionist running dog

it doesn't say much   it says

WE GATHER TO LOVINGLY REMEMBER

Stanley John (Stan) Czerwonka

BORN   **DIED**
August 21st, 1971   October 28th, 2013
Vernon, British Columbia

CREMATION

CELEBRATION OF STAN'S LIFE
10:00 A.M.
Monday, November 4th, 2013
Bethel Funeral Chapel
Vernon, British Columbia

OFFICIATING CLERGY
Reverend Father Donald Newton

INTERMENT
Czerwonka Family Plot
Pleasant Valley Cemetery
Vernon, British Columbia

some stuff on the back   address of the chapel
short impersonal message beginning *On behalf of the family*
note in the bottom righthand corner   *printed in USA, ©1994*
stuff like that

on the front   corny picture   ocean sunset

& on the inside   left-hand side   picture of Stan
latter-day Stan   balding   smiling just a little   wearing
what looks like a tuxedo   not sure why or when

underneath the picture it says
"Sweetness Follows"
which I might be responsible for   it's an REM song we both liked   maybe I mentioned it to somebody

though I never would've used fucking quotation marks
or   for that matter   put fucking *Stan* in parentheses
in the middle of his name or included a message   on behalf of the family
when they were all fucking dead anyway

3599 pleasant valley road

Dad said he'd been in what used to be
Stan's house. A carpenter friend of his
who builds movie sets bought it
from the estate & renovated the inside
but left the exterior mostly intact,
1970s stucco & brick & wrought-iron railings
I still feel in my hand, winter-cold,
decades later. When they cleaned out the house
after Stan died I got boxes of his books, China,
KISS, the collection of Dazai Osamu short stories
I sent him, my first book, dedicated & signed
to him, & I found old school photos
from Bearisto Elementary in an envelope, golden
Stan fat-cheeked at 7 or 8 & not even past.
The carpenter sent me a fancy drone video
of the house, made for advertising purposes.
A shot of the front yard from the sidewalk
I walked ten thousand times. New rooms.
The stairs reversed so that now they start
at the edge of the kitchen instead of off
the living room, flipping my sense
of things. The upstairs all modern-sleek,
Mrs C's pizzas on the stove or Stan shouting
in her deaf kitchen ears long-gone. The freshly painted
hallways, once full of indescribable nameless junk
meant for poorer relations back in Poland.
Stan's old bedroom: unrecognizable. The spare
room I slept in once or twice. The living
room where his dad told us hysterical stories
about the venereal disease champion of the Polish army
& we screamed with laughter. The downstairs
entirely altered. Spaces where we gabbled,
dug Beatles, roared, sported eyeball to eyeball, gone.
A world within the world, endless & dense.
But the outside's still the same except for the stairs
to the deck, which are gone, & the kitchen door
I used to knock on & through which I'd see
Stan coming through from the living room
preliminary to cutting out for a walk or the Kal.
The little translucent curtain that hung in the window.
Pleasant Valley Cemetery a kilometre or two to the north,

Stan & his parents there under the leaves & snow.
Nothing looks the same on the outside
anymore. I sure don't. But Stan's house,
full of strangers, full of ghosts, unaccountably does,
though the world within is defunct & dead
except in me, just as vast
inside as out.

this is the thanks you get

    about matching the man to his coffin
    Jack Spicer said

      one must maim him to fit him in

    drowsical Thursday afternoon
    my desk in the staff room at work
    Ginan Junior High School, Ginan Town
    the room where I learned you were dead

    office noise then as now more or less

    (can you see me fumbling undeft
    & busy maiming what you were?
    with all these words & me
    & not enough truth or you?)

    the information coming via Facebook fall 2013
    from Geoff in Vernon:
    jason you should know stan passed
    about an hour ago

    ego noise then as now more or less

    (or like who cares about two non-macho guys
    who loved each other for 30 years
    & had a few small adventures here & there
    as described by the mournful one still alive later?)

    & three years after on October 28
    which is incidentally
    the date of your death
    I'm flying to Beijing

    money from your estate
    paying for the trip
    to go & see some of
    the things you saw

but 16 years too late
to see you there
for which I'm sorrier
than you'll ever know

roving

in ghostly zimbabwe

    our ghosts in the rainbirds hauling storms
        over great houses of stone near Masvingo
    our ghosts in Mugabe's motorcade, a million cops & soldiers, he's dead now
        at last & no sorrow attaches to his name
    our ghosts in the bulldozers starting up in township bleaks,
        Zimbabwean bulldozers! & wreckage near & far, be glad
            you aren't poor, ghost
    our ghosts in Zimbabwe coming down wrong
    our ghosts in beer garden with my host father Phil
        drinking bucket beer eating fried beetles yelling talk
            in fever-tree starstalk thumb piano dark, every sound African,
            the moon too, & Phil dead
                already now, his kids married, scattered,
                    friendly still
    our ghosts in jacaranda circus & lightning strike
    our ghosts in bush war not even past
    our ghosts in the elephant behind the cabin at the river, colossal skull-swing,
        mutual surprise & getaway, tourist gored only
            a week before, elephants fast in bursts 60 kms per hour
    our ghosts in generous red township dust
        & wild foosball under awnings
    our ghosts sneaking school uniform smokes at Christian Brothers College eludin
        sinister prefects with Andy, he's in
            Uganda now, safari business, go see him someday
    our ghosts in Life brand cigarettes, Madison cigarettes, jars
        of brandy, halfjacks of cane, elephant-skin hipflask, our ghosts drunk
            on the plane back from Malawi
    our ghosts in roaring cataract, linked by vapours & fall
    our ghosts in witch doctor hut, his juggled bones & dust indicate
        I'll marry Lucille & be back some day
    our ghosts of Portuguese blowjob in backseat, of diamond cock
        on the corner, of one
            lonely fuck
    our ghosts in Haddon & Sly, reflected in Bulawayo windows, my ghost with stack
        of crappy poems to show Josephine in Pizzaghetti
    our ghosts hitchhiking to Marondera, to KweKwe, to Harare & never once afraid
    our ghosts in crocodile slam, hippo shit, flying ants, in the little springbok
        that leapt & saw us & twisted mid-air came down wrong
            & we all heard his leg pop broken & the guide
                said dead by nightfall lions'll get him

our ghosts in Zambezi canoe yelling for weed from raggedy guys on Zambian side
our ghosts with streetwalkers on ouzo sidewalks, our ghosts
        on nighttime Trade Fair rooftop talking not talking
our ghosts in disarray, our ghosts harmonized
our ghosts in October wailing the rain down beautiful
our ghosts gleeful projecting Hippo Gypsy jubilation into the future
        forever
                without check

london (just as vast inside as out)

before back to Vernon   to see Lucille   see Stan
after a year of Hippo Gypsy capers in Zimbabwe & Malawi   in Swaziland
& South Africa   desert & river & elephant & ouzo & Soweto dusk-fuming
Church & I plan 2 weeks in the UK   maybe hitchhike to Paris?
unafraid as that
change our flights   & plunge into London   world city   world-pearl

all goes wrong-shaped fast   money failure fuck-up
spend the last of our cash on a bottle   fill our heads with wine
in St James's Park   wonder what to do   where to go
the dreadful city roaring all around wants to eat us   convert us
into rubble & ash
into ghosts

pauperized in a day   down to panhandling & humiliation
all over the place   Royal Albert Hall   Abbey Road   Whitechapel
two eighteen-year-olds of the abyss   continual tramp & try
no beer at the Black Lamb for us   no gin at the Owl Bowl   no whiskey
at The Maid in the Moon   no monkey dancing on a tambourine
no boar-baiting   no waxworks
just pressure-shadows   & crisscrossing the city
the struggle for survival   in the mouth of the ravening monster metropolis
flopping wherever we can   Hyde Park   churchyard   Victoria Station
grateful recipients of Christian Aid for the Homeless   coffee & sandwiches

call our grandmothers   ask them to wire us some money
get a bottle & get drunk in magic lantern streets
but start contending   sick of each other   sick of beggary
nearly fight right there   on a sidewalk by a hedge   until some guy
looking for combat action   comes at us with a broken bottle
has time to punch me   once   hard
before a cop car comes round the corner

finally Church flies home to Wisconsin   back to his own ghosts & grind
while I walk Trafalgar Square with a broken nose
just want to go home   can barely believe in it   a fridge with food
shower   bed   family breathing asleep in the warm quiet house
see if Lucille still loves me   & tell Stan my stories
on renewed walks around the town he hasn't left yet

& so back to Vernon   but only stay a month
have to keep moving   too used to too much freedom
& bored of that fridge fast   take off for Tofino
for Banff   for staff accommodations & hash & filth
my sun-flooded Africa & dizzy London long gone far off
& me no longer the international jet-set hero   novel & strange
just some guy   not even home

poland (just as vast inside as out)

Railroad Amsterdam to Katowice
via Berlin & Wroclaw. Longest day.
Sinister train sounds in the vast November
black. Bloodlands. Forgot
to change money, hungry all the way.

My brother'd said *Keep your wits about you, the popular thing
now is to chloroform tourists, if you're not careful
you'll wake up naked in St Petersburg. Also be careful
you don't get off at the wrong stop, beware North Katowice, New Katowice,
Central Katowice, Old Katowice.*

An ugly drunk in the final compartment browbeats
everybody, bellows Polish, plays shit music
on his shit cassette player. I creep
carefully into the corridor. Open
the window. Mingle my breath with the rushing dark.

Fall out at the final station hungry thirsty tired
& there he is on the steps. My little brother. Smiling.
In his high-ceilinged apartment he makes dinner,
makes tea, plays Dylan's *Up to Me*.
My first time. We sit smoking, bent to the music.

Two days later an ex-nun drives us to Auschwitz.
Brick chimneys in Birkenau's bleak plain. Polish skies.
All of it. My smallness. And the weather
is awful. I read later that's what
everybody says. It's always awful there.

Krakow. In the square St Mary's trumpet call's cut off
by a Mongol arrow in 1241. Photo of
my brother & me & the dragon Smock Wawelski.
On the train back to Berlin a man looks exactly
like my father, right down to the sweater.

Stan: your father from Kurki, your mother
from Suchowola. Where? Villages
with both names all over Poland.
More mystery & gap. Your erasure
accelerating. My loss getting bigger.

You went to Poland as a kid on a trip
& didn't want to go back to Canada.
Told your mom your dad would get over
you eventually. This is where you come from.
Where it started. And I myself am not over you.

in ghostly mexico

      my ghost one among many over Gulf, rescued
         from Miami shopping mall murders,
            far away, flying, hauling my associate ghosts
               with me like Whitman's old delicious burdens,
      my ghost small & weak but bolstered by sidekick ghosts,
         comrades, chinas, amigos
      my ghost flowing southward to Mexico just like that,
         paying 70 pesos to downtown Mérida, past old paint through warm dust
          & dozy repose in the plaza, in the cathedral lambent at dusk
      my ghost a Rain God with an elephant face & a coachwhip snake
         coming out of my mouth & a human face coming
            out of the snake's mouth &
               eyes like cenotes full of jawbones & jade
      my ghost passing under ancient cold arch full of Mayan light, moaning
         on jaguar throne, my ghost limping to the bus station at dawn
      my ghost talking with cab driver about Cancun bullfighting, he sez
         "Ees bullsheet"— kids yelling Olé! at the skullbash ring—gore
            for whooping tourists from Idaho, my ghost in the blood
               in the sand
      my ghost calling the front desk for any problem, decomposition, or disturb
      my ghost nothing more than a fossilized plankton crybaby full of soul-doubt
         bedazzled in a dream of conception meat & a stretch of dark
            towards Cuba
      my ghost yakking all day with 2 sexy women from Rotterdam
      my ghost reading Dickens poolside, whiter than when I started
      my ghost on top of a pyramid in the middle of jungle sea,
         my own beating heart a lamp to light the dim & mist &
            clear away the fear
      my ghost padding softfoot at sunset down a street on the Island of Women
         seeing right into darkish living rooms, kids asleep
            in hammocks, murmurs, faintness, unilluminated tenderness, all
               history compressed to a single domestic point
      my ghost planning to bring my girl here someday on honeymoon
         but that'll never happen, all that's doomed too
      my ghost a bowl of lime soup & a wobble of monkey water
      my ghost aiming Aztec telescopes at eternity, searching for eternal tristesse
      my ghost is just a horny weirdo crockashit afoot in the world & already
         bending to be one ghost among many rushing
            through upper air back to worklife hassles in Japan
      my ghost farewelling all the ghosts I saw & met in Mex—Cancun bar
         lisping cynic—French girl at Uxmal—street musician

>wiping rain off his guitar—little curio kid gnawing
>>on the plaster knee of a
>>>crucified Christ
>>>>in the middle of the
>>>>>noise

how to enjoy your trip to china

      run your breath through your toes, see what it teaches you

          observe the sounds

      let a hundred flowers bloom, let a hundred thoughts contend

          shut the fuck up for once

      leave no traces

          bombard the headquarters

      accept all goofy awkwardness & flunk forever

          get a little closer

beijing (just as vast inside as out)

    this is boundless place
    beat up & weird like Zimbabwe:
    ancient bike repair, wreckage rubble,
    human wreckage, traffic babble, full colour & blast

    cut out walking with Patrick past
    hutong alleys, power meter mysteries,
    wires tangled crazy, impossible doorways,
    dim impossible lights

    gangs of guys
    pickaxing all the streets to pieces
    just like Mexico
    in the flashing dark

    go down long orange wall
    to Tiananmen Square in the morning
    under blue Chinese sky
    through plainclothes air

    yokels from the provinces
    holding three-yuan flowers
    bow at the statue of the
    most beloved Great Helmsman

    the Forbidden City is
    endless imperial space
    & old men in Mao caps
    don't give a shit

    cold willows
    bend over water,
    hungry ghosts, edible nests,
    & phantom tanks

    walk back to hotel alone
    down Changan Avenue
    Hi! Where you from? You kiss me? says a girl
    in dowager shadow

later walking drunk to Village Bar
Patrick & I sort out our
personality problems forever,
know we have to be in our bodies

fully accepting & kind,
self-forgiven, accommodating, humorous,
with all oddball awkwardness & flop
included forever while we

look at the flowers from our
galloping horses, our horses
of Liverpool, Tokyo, Cape Town, Gifu,
Paris, Vernon, Poland, Berlin

beyond the spray of graves,
talk, trifles, travel, rooms
& all the lines we crossed
to be right here now

song dynasty governmental ministries

ministry of punishment

ministry of sparrows

ministry of armed struggle

ministry of wine

ministry of gratitude

ministry of suicide

ministry of contradictions among the people

ministry of temptation

ministry of torture

ministry of longing

ministry of pearls in snow

ministry of basic identity

ministry of adolescent belligerence

ministry of early morning befuddlement

ministry of ultimate reality

ministry of decay

ministry of unrememberable erotics

ministry of resistance

ministry of protracted nostalgia

ministry of middle-aged regret

ministry of the spheres of grief

tiananmen square

    Max & I go & stand in the square. Tiananmen
    means *Gate of Heavenly Peace*,
    as everybody knows. Biggest square
    in the world. Or most people, anyway.
    Mao's mausoleum. Mao mostly wax, or gone.

    Nobody clobbers & hauls us
    panic-struggling into the Forbidden City
    for decapitation. Nobody ships our corpses
    to Shanghai for cremation. Nobody knows
    who Tank Man was, or if he's gone or what.

    But how many students shot & mangled
    thirty years ago now? Workers too. *The people love*
    the army, the army loves the people! We were
    in high school & didn't care about China. At least
    I didn't. Gone. All gone anyway.

    See the sun & wind & space
    & tour guides trailing clouds of bucolics
    from Jiangxi province & Taishan. You
    were here, Stan, & bought me a Mao lighter that
    flashed & beeped. We are here & you are gone.

observe the sounds

    my sons breathing asleep

    things have changed, the east is red, what'll I do

    clattering ghosts of Tiananmen dead

    the noise in the middle of the pearl

    crash of Mongol wind on the Wall

    endless background roar of fuss & distress

    Chinese mountains & rivers happening

the 4 pests

    Under the jewel-centre of the Celestial Throne
    on Coal Hill in Beijing
    the last Ming emperor hangs himself
    & his shadow makes a wind-monkey
    that slowly swings & drinks the wind.

    Under the nine layers of heaven
    on an island in the Pearl River
    in a room cooled by tubs of ice
    the Great Helmsman sits burning incense
    & eating the ashes.

    Under the thousand stars, the thousand suns,
    in a shack made of suncloud & ice-pure
    beneath the wall, among chattering ghosts,
    our words freeze & hang in the air
    & stay like that until spring.

    Under the skin of eternity
    on Worker Peasant Soldier Street
    we crash our cymbals & smash our pots
    so that none of the sparrows can land till at last
    they drop exhausted & dead from the sky.

last day in beijing

drinking seven-yuan beers
last hour Day's Inn Forbidden City
— hangover in sullen abeyance

Max back to work
Patrick already gone
& a billion Chinese don't care

```
                (2 stops)              (3 stops)                  Airport
Wongfujing ——————— Jianguomen ——————Dongzhimen ——Express
 (Line 1)                              (Line 2)
```

leaving China
last half Xanax Max gave me
dissolving in bloodstream

waitress gives me
a hard face & a
glass of hot water

fall asleep
don't wake up till Nagoya
& of course it's raining

read *Dharma Bums* to Gifu
get a can & walk down Keyaki-dori
open my door

home from China
Maho dozing under the *kotatsu*
everything in its place

Joe & Sasha healthy upstairs asleep
& Joe passed his swimming test
like a champ

in ghostly china

    Stan I know your ghost's in China, I went looking for it & found it
    Your ghost in vast cold Tiananmen Square yokel space
           in the summer full of tanks
                in Forbidden City gift shop
                      in seahorse steam, your ghost a starfish on a stick
    Your ghost in willowy park yelling No photo!
    Your ghost in wind ripped from Inner Mongolia
           in castration knot
                in *hutong* tangle dim light impossible
                      in Mao's crystal coffin corpse a waxy fake
                          in village bar actually called Village Bar
    Your ghost in the Fall
           in suspended particulates
                in my grenade-shaped booze bottle at the foot of the Wall
                      in the Central Commission for Discipline Inspection
                          in ceaseless loss & defeat
    Your ghost in winter iron
           in our hangovers on the subway
                in springtime opium smog
                     in revisionist criminal rightists & capitalist roaders
                        in the Four Treasures of the Study
                            in hang-glider wheelbarrow
                                firecracker chess
    Your ghost in the character for destruction
            in Little Red Book I bought 45 *yuan*
                in my phantom Xanax sleep flying home
    Your ghost in my kids' sleeping foreheads I kiss upstairs
    Your ghost I went looking for & found
           in China of all places
              Stan

went to find you

went to China

went to find you

got a little closer

can't seal the book

can't loosen my grip

but now maybe I

can light my lamp

strap you on &

walk your corpse

over the hills

over the wall

& home

japan

watching home movies ten years later #1

Credit screen says *Based on a baby
created by Jason & Maho*. Born 7 October at 5:38 pm,
50 cms long & 3355 grams. Joe, 30 seconds old,
his trembling mouth, & outside
deep autumn light. O tenderness.

In the incubator, looking around, looking right
at me looks like, though from what I've read he can't
see me that far through two sheets of glass
& his tears & mine. In another room they sew
Maho up where she tore or where the doctor undid her.

Unfilmed: my jubilant ride home from
hospital across Kinka Bridge over the
Nagara River through cool fall dark,
exultant, transported, gloating over my joy. Never
fell in love so fast & now my heart is full,

Joe instantly plugging the Canada-shaped hole
in me because what's daylight savings time,
Northern Lights, Empress Hotel, Kalamalka
Lake, Davison Orchards & ready access to
Kraft Dinner & weed compared to this?

Text screen says *Maho & Joe move into the Nakahara Building
& Jason instantly reverts to a swinging bachelor lifestyle*
which I didn't at all, got up at 5:30 to get to Sakahogi
on time for work, sun-slanted trains out there, the Kiso
River, fields, & nighttime reading *Ulysses*.

Common in Japan to move in with your parents
after a kid, help with everything & Maho's parents
& grandmother live five minutes away.
I stop over after work & boxing. Joe
touches my face with his fist.

Many things suddenly making perfect sense.
Much has changed. World has changed.
I want to call my mother on the phone
& forgive her & beg forgiveness. O
tenderness backwards in time, & now.

And then the day: Joe brought home at last.
Triumphant Beethoven emperor music but what
am I saving my joyful Beatles for? Anyroad:
here he is, on his back in the crib, moving his arms
& legs, wonderstruck at the mobile turning above.

& I thought 7 years was a long time

    shoulda mastered money
    & rain by now   but

    after tomorrow's tomorrow's tomorrow
    something is old

    all started with students
    flinging finger-hearts

    what I remember
    when I remember

    thumb & index together   & raised
    & say *kyun desu*

    "the sound of your heart"
    beating lush in the chest

    drove me home her car her
    white shirt the ice

    when I remember
    something is old

    dim-eyed in a dark
    her white shirt in the dark

    freight a finger with heart-fall
    send it nearer   also back

    towards her gift
    a freshening   a feel thing

    when lush was the word
    & flop was the colour

    my old fingers now
    going *kyun* in the hallway

    girls the same age
    as when lush was the word

white shirt in the dark
a free feel thing

when my fingers could summon
a lushness & damp

heartbound & how
to remember   remember

my fangs
in the dark   rushing to linger

the small hearts I made
with this & that finger

I have tenderly adulterous thoughts

           sometimes, mostly
going backwards, lovers
from before, breasts
from before, faces, scenes—
does everybody do this?
Rewind long-gone
erotic triumphs, revive the famous
orgasms still smoking
in memory, fresh bomb craters,
volcanoes, pylons on fire, that one
time, the other time, every
interesting time with
her or both or whoever?
Or maybe animate some present improbability,
the beautifully plain girl in the post office,
the stunner briefly glimpsed buying coffee
in the Mini Stop?
But these are just the happy thoughts
of an idle man, the distant silent throb
of a pulsar in a corner of the universe, far away.
Because when I'm sleeping & some molten
scorcher, all tongue & tits,
is ready & hungry & says so,
shows me, I tend to fret & demur
because I'm very married to you
even in my dreams,
sweetheart.

camping at katsura beach in kochi prefecture

Perfect crescent curve
of shoreline—
rocky promontory
with tiny *torii* shrine atop
to the right, left
a lower out-jut of rock,
sea-carved, easily climbed.

The lighthouse & moon above
sweeping in eternity,
down here my father & I
tired in our tents
set back among winded trees
100 metres from
the rush of the water on the land.

Sounds of fishing boats
further out in the Pacific dark
& click & whistle chatter from
the cheapjack aquarium,
dolphins & seals
talking to each other
all night in their pools.

My father & I also talking
back & forth, from
tent to tent, between
the trees, up the beach
from the blue foaming shore,
not even halfway through our
1200-kilometre pilgrimage walk

but curving slowly, perfectly,
along Kochi's coast,
a little cheapjack ourselves,
comradely, humorous,
& down already to
basic things. Moon, rock,
water, talk.

watching home movies ten years later #2

Got hipped to Ray at last by Cohen,
an interview where he talks about playing
"You Win Again" over & over again, in Greece.
And I dutifully checked it out & fell in love
with that one & all the rest.

Gracious me: Joe's gorgeous angelic
period. People stop us on the street to peer in at
him & coo. "Half?" they ask, meaning half-Japanese,
but I'm not bothered & Maho doesn't care though
some people think it should be *Double* instead.

Take a train through the valleys with my dad,
visiting from Vernon. Gero: hot spring town.
Steaming river pools, snow here & there. Fine,
quiet feelings. Gold flakes frittered over
our hotel dinners. Beers & talk in the room.

Joe quite vocal now, *eh-eh-eh-eh*, his little mouthful
of music. Everyone holding him. My son
in everyone's arms. My son
in my father's arms, & Joe talking to him
eh-eh-eh!

Christmas in our Gifu room, Joe on my father's lap.
Dad examining the copy of Ken Kesey's
Sometimes a Great Notion I got him.
Ray Charles in the room too. This
is happiness. Paste it in your memory show.

Long hours editing & burning DVDs, thought
it would be a drag without smoking but it's fine,
like everything else. Walk to the post office
to send copies to Canada, to my brother
& sister, old girlfriends, best pal Stan.

But will all that work & time, time away
from Maho & Joe, even last? Or last for long?
My little cave paintings? My family maps? Technology,
decay, earthquakes, decline. Joe's story written
on tree bark, rice paper, water, snow. Mine & Maho's, too.

things to do around gifu
    after Gary Snyder

Ramble down Tamamiya Street to the Bier Hall get good & drunk on credit
¥100 water pistols in the park
Nanamagari Trail up Mt Kinka to the castle
Walk the Nagara River from bridge to bridge
Meet Tom at Masa for a bench beer & chat
Groan hungover biking to work
Hit a baseball out of Hongo Park & conk a parked car
Read neon-sweet wolf-eye-green Sheri Benning poems
Notebooks & dried flowers at Koti, pens & envelopes from Loft
Screw your lover at The Dolphin, The Zoo, Seven Hilton, Olympia
Acupuncture for your tinnitus
Modern Love Ticket to Ride C'mon & Love Me How Soon
    Is Now? at Shidax karaoke with Patrick Black
Stock up on Strong Zero lemon-flavoured 9% chu-hai at Family Mart
Get your hair cut by your brother-in-law at Vernon, named after your old village
Media Cosmos library take out *Madame Bovary* again don't read it again
Celestial assistance at Inaba Shrine
Squirrels at Squirrel Village
Turn in your documents at City Hall get married to Maho
Cha-han & gyoza & ramen at Osho
Get up early clean the neighbourhood with neighbours
Send postcards to Vernon Vancouver Cranbrook Winnipeg Toronto
    Haida Gwai & Prattville, Alabama
Wave at Victoria waiting for the bus
Float by ghost remnants of Rollo's & remember
Buy a white necktie at Brick House for weekend wedding work
Kiss your kids good morning goodnight
Make plans to leave
Make plans to stay

big penis

Some of the more uninhibited
boys at the school where I work
like to ask me sex-related questions
at the back of the class, trying
out their proudly filthy vocab
on the lowly assistant English
teacher. Junior high. Thirteen,
fourteen. You can imagine.
One of them will sidle up
& ask, *Jason sensei*
big penis? And I answer
Giant, which they think
is hilarious. *Yappari ne,*
somebody says—I thought so.
Jason sensei, sex yatta koto aru?
Have you ever had sex? And I remind them
I've got two kids. It takes them
a while to put it together
& then they whoop & yell.
Jason sensei had sex! Two times!
Then more porno stuff,
do I like big *oppai,* how about
blowjobs, etc. Giggling
questions about my
meagre sexual credentials which
I duck & deflect best I can.
Or maybe not meagre, I
don't know. A few tender
myths, a few triumphant
flops. But comparisons are
odious & the mysteries
remain & the questions
keep coming, sleazier
all the time, & the
giggling too. Meanwhile
the girls, pens in
the air,
listen, quietly.

watching home movies ten years later #3

Biking & filming around Gifu. *Ukai*
boats & the river. Buying an elephant
shirt for born-in-time Joe at a
market at the station. Looking better
on video than I do in real life.

Mia, daughter of the guy through whom
I met Maho, gently slapping Joe's head
& passing him her pacifier. Ten years
later they're in the same class
at Meigo Elementary

where Joe seems intimidated
or maybe just not interested in girls yet though
he had a thing for Kumi-chan in kindergarten.
I was interested when I was ten: Tawnya & Trish,
Debbie & Stephanie, & all the rest.

Maho, backlit, holding Joe.
If not for her. Her scars & flexure,
her knock-kneed walk. Her body
feeding our baby. I'd be nowhere at all
without our intermingling drift.

Should write an Ode to Our Genitals
for the good job they've done here.
For the concord & rain-swept
blankets, for little clutching shudders.
For Joe, who can now drag himself along.

cosmopolitan scenes: junior high school

A volleyball on the roof in the rain.

Ten umbrellas in the stand at the end of the hall.

The school nurse, sniffing in the staff room.

Non-colour of the sky at 9:52 a.m.

Six students, all boys, sleeping through second period English.

Saori tickling Satoshi with a pen.

Suzuki sensei's shirt: *I NEVER FLAT UNDER ANY PRESSURE*

Yumi with *hachimaki*—headband—written on her forearm.

The window frame in 2-3 making a shadow stripe down Momoko's back.

Breeze through the window of the 4th floor tatami room as I read & nap.

Tatsuya sketching a dinosaur biting another dinosaur's tail on his handou

Ayumi fanning Aya with a green pencil board.

A pen case in 2-2: *Cute Diner ACTION Go! Sweet Candy Girls!*

Yuri's pen case: *Don't Stop Pretty.*

The janitor choking on his lunch for the second day in a row.

watching home movies ten years later #4

Opening: Morrissey, from when we all went
to see him at Club Zepp: "Nagoya, my heart is full."
Clips treated to look like the video for
How Soon Is Now? Joe on a train, killer whale,
dolphins, penguins, lightning over Gifu, eclipse.

Maho, when I ask her what appeals to her
about Morrissey, says "I like his—pronunciation."
She's pregnant again. Tom, drunk, gesturing
at a map on my wall: "Fuck off, Russia! Fucking
hold your head in shame!" He hates Dostoevsky too.

Joe afoot in the neighbourhood, looking in storm
drains & pointing. *Dog! Apple!* Maho carries him
over to where our neighbour has a little Santa figurine
on his mailbox & Joe says "Bumpa, hello!"
Bumpa: what all the grandchildren call my dad.

Joe reading *Man Gave Names to All the Animals*,
looking for Goldbug in *Cars & Trucks & Things That Go*.
An improvised restaurant: Joe's Malt Stop.
He pours invisible drinks from cup to cup, brings me
one, gives one to his slingshot monkey.

Sometimes I get sad watching these movies, sad about Joe,
mourn upcoming losses, brutality of the world, all
the things in the future waiting to hurt him, squabbles,
pointlessness, miscarriages, breast cancer, uppercuts.
All now goof & discovery. His hopeless happiness.

Or maybe it's not Joe's losses, but mine. Anhedonic
fears. Age come to wither me & crone Maho. Joe's interest
in things set against my own drifting. Maybe.
But all that's inside, unshown. In the end, no music
playing, me in a Morrissey shirt, packing for Canada.

And so to my old village for my brother's wedding.
He doesn't know Maho & Joe are coming too.
Missed my sister's wedding, missed my mother's
death, need to stop missing things. And here's Joe
becoming a worldwide person.

Drive along the lakes & O my heart. Down College Drive
to Dad's house. Family chatter on the deck. A pack
of aunts & uncles. The phone's for me:
my old pal Geoff. Cousins taking good care
of Joe. Gambols on the neighbour's lawn.

Backyard wedding. John Lent playing guitar &
I tear up watching, now. Why? Didn't at the time.
September lake beyond, the bride's Brazilian
family, Rod singing *Born in Time*.
And suddenly Stan, right next to me.

Joe: naked in Kal Lake, feeding a goat
at Davison Orchards, falling asleep
at pizza table. Sprinkler sounds. "You guys
have so much nature!" says Maho. Sun
setting over Okanagan hills.

Maho & Dad & Joe & I go out to Coldstream graveyard
to visit Mum. *Komorebi:* light filtered through trees.
Joe picking dandelions among the headstones.
The look Dad gives me before walking off—
what does it mean? Stop filming me when I'm sad?

Talking about KISS in the Kal Hotel bar with Stan,
just like the old golden days. Last time I'll see
him. He picked up something in China or gave up or
his heart broke bleak & he'll die next year
& I'll miss that too.

you will go

> I am contained in this body;
> all of us move in the spheres of our grief
> our private joys. Look at the mailman and his dizzying
> happiness, the housewife next door, her heart a trembling needle
> — Sarah Tsiang, "You Are Gone"

When you die Dad I'll have a particular private Japanese
sadness all to myself, your vapor anchored
to my concretes here—my couch, the castle, Kyoto, Kochi,
my street, my desk, blue mountains, the river, big table
in Bier Hall, the sake shop, graveyard on Koya, Nara, Nikko,
Tokyo with its dazzling pulse, giddy, gaudy.
Temple to temple and mountain to mountain when we
walked a thousand Shikoku kilometres—fussing with ghosts
even then: your wife, my mother, loosed, disembodied.
I am contained in this body

and you in yours but you'll be loosed too—to
international saddening—heat, ash, the ceremonies
that stitch pain to the future. What's to be done? Nobody
knows. So we drink and read, bend to connect
head to head to help, to hear, to touch when we can.
Our mouths with their talking, maps, pain, Dief the Chief,
the stars in their wheeling, Tarantula Nebula, lightning on
Jupiter, your days in the Navy, the girls unkissed, the mill, the past—
but it's ok if we never could provide the final rim of relief:
all of us move in the spheres of our grief.

Around us the many, neighbours, spiders, salesmen, sons,
Joe with his singing—*Here comes the sun*—Sasha calling
for bananas at bedtime, the ceaseless sewing of our lives
together, and always the chance to notice, accept, pause
in astonishment—the needle stilled—like when Maho looks,
stops, says "This is happiness." Self-pitying
doesn't deliver and fear is the killer, which leaves us with
what? The compass needle quivers, points to distant blues.
It won't last but being happy is this: unashamedly feeling
our private joys. Look at the mailman with his dizzying.

When you're dead you'll be scattered freely to flow over
my map, ghost-marked, daily encountered, closer
than ever, maybe closer than now. Who knows? Wind through
pine tree branches, lightning on the castle, a grief, a
pause, unintegrated, vast, broken into joys spent in sprees with me
here, and here, and here. Chances to be gleeful, the Beatles
and travel, books and wine, loss transformed into visions
beautiful with that blue. Letting go with a laugh.
No more achievement, no more struggling to be heedful.
Happiness, the housewife next door, her heart a trembling needle.

watching home movies ten years later #5

    Joe careens through the mall to McCartney's
Too Many People. Everything he says & does
is an overburst, an adore. "Blue Meanie! Old Fred!"
or "More snake!" Sasha overdue, Maho's distension
unsettling, the world within her.

    Takahashi Ladies Clinic. I'm reading Doris Andersen's
Slave of the Haida, elementary school fave rave,
in Maho's room. A foot-long needle goes into her arm
to get Sasha to come out. I slip away
for a beer & nearly miss everything.

    Sasha appears, enormous, healthy, blood
in the curl of his ear. He makes Buddha mudras
with his fingers & now begins a new phase in our lives.
One night later I'm in Nagoya with Tim & Tom
to see Ringo Starr at Club Zepp.

    McCartney music: *I don't want no other baby but you.*
A bit obvious but perfect for long shots of Sasha
on the squirm & yawn & frown in his crib.
Joe leans in to kiss him & Sasha burps in his face.
The little sore on his lip from sucking on Maho.

    A spring-froth of cherry blossoms & below
a baby, my baby. Petals in a pond, in the gutter.
Joe reading a book about trains: "Oh look!
I love this train! Babies take this train!"
The smell of our rooms. Our happiness.

    "What colour are your eyes, Joe?" "Brown."
"What colour are Dada's eyes?" "Green!"
"What colour are Mama's eyes?" "Mama is black."
"Black eyes?" "Yes!" "What colour are
Sasha's eyes?" "Sasha—just monster eyes."

Winter cold-light, Cole Porter songs, a crane
in the river, Dylan Thomas talking about knocking
his brother down at Christmastime. Sasha & Joe
& general crashbangings on the couch. Joe yelling
about Santa, Sasha tumbling off the table.

My sons, attached through sympathy & private
language codes & kitchen memories & mine
& Maho's blood sealed in their skulls.
All the travel & talk to come. Brothers to swap
their secret visions down through time.

earthquake

    earthquake crashing in the brain of the crow on the roof
    earthquake swimming in the sheets of my bed
    earthquake trembling in the cicada's wing
    earthquake on the moon
    earthquake chattering in the middle of my guilt
    earthquake opening in the eye of the sun
    earthquake glimmering inside the torpedo
    earthquake running through the bride, through the ring
    earthquake with its load of jacaranda & trains
    earthquake in the table
    earthquake all wrong
    earthquake arriving too early too late
    earthquake pouring from the guts of the flower
    earthquake leaping from the cactus spike
    earthquake appearing in the heart of the typhoon
    earthquake bent in the rocks under Gifu, waiting
        to take my family away

watching home movies ten years later #6

Two buses, three trains, & the funicular to the top
of Mt Koya in Wakayama-ken. Worldwide
diamond-centre of Shingon Buddhism & eternal
meditative retreat of Kobo Daishi, ancient saint.
Kids & Maho & Maho's folks. My fourth visit.

We stay at Fukuchi-in temple. Rocks
& raked sand. Dragon in the ceiling. Celestials
everywhere. At the end of town: the biggest
burial ground in Japan. In a dream
Kobo Daishi tells Joe, "Buddha is a big guy."

The Webb sisters singing *If It Be Your Will* & wind
humming in the graveyard's cryptomeria trees. Lanterns.
Moss-light. Sasha in the carrier on my back. The rock
Kobo Daishi is said to have rested on. Joe
collecting twigs & branches. Cohen's rags of light.

Ask a monk to write Stan's name on a grave tablet
& Joe picks a Kannon Boddhisattva statue. Lord
of Compassion, Goddess of Mercy. We place the *toba*
in a little container & pour water from the
Jewel Stream over it & splash the statue as well.

For Stan. For Stan. For the shatter-cone in my heart.
After dark I'll come back alone & bury a picture
of Stan as close to the Daishi's crypt as I can get. Crypt,
or cottage—the monks still bring him food twice a day.
In there a thousand years & not even dead.

All these people, all these lives, all the ashes
carried from across Japan for interment close to the
great saint. The charnel house behind the Lantern Hall.
My sons yelling "No!" at each other & laughing,
laughing, down the path through the graves.

taken to private areas & harmed

    thwarted by typhoons & no ferry
    to Aka Island till maybe tomorrow
    we rent a car & drive
    to the Former Japanese
    Navy Underground
    Headquarters—

    Okinawa means
    rope over the sea

    —hacked deep in the hill in '44 by soldiers
    with pickaxes & hoes & rope
    baskets for hauling
    the dirt to the surface,
    450 meters & no
    toilets

    & now here comes the Typhoon of Steel:
    half a million Americans with guns,
    black-out, bombardment, the noise the noise,
    the island on fire

    reverse slope corkscrew
    & blowtorch, crows
    of smoke, sweet-potato brandy
    for the Emperor's birthday.

    Staff officer's room:
    shrapnel-spattered wall & a sign that says
    jiketsu sareta toki no teryudan no dankon
    which is translated as
    WALL RIDDLED WITH A HAND-GRENADE
    WHEN COMMITTED SUICIDE

    —I put my finger in a shrapnel hole
    just like I touched
    a bullet hole in Berlin
    busted-up crematorium remains in Birkenau
    napalm-scorched stone lantern in Gifu
    the air in Tiananmen Square—

& down the final hall & through the final door
with a homemade spear, a bayonet lashed
to a stick
to die with an American bullet in your eye
& lie under a screwpine
forever—corpses so abundant that
when walking at night civilians
carry wooden sticks
so as not to step on
dead bodies
in the dark

Scraped flat by the roller
wrote Sylvia Plath
of wars, wars, wars

Rear Admiral Ota wrote
a telegram in the tunnel
& sent it to the Navy Vice Admiral
& said
This battle is nearing its end
There are no trees, no grass
Everything is burnt to the ground

even Joe with his jalopy energies
is subdued down here
in the old-tooth light
& flicker-drip

throw me a rope
sang Gillian Welch
on the rolling tide

the tunnels are
not far from Hacksaw Ridge
not far from Shuri Castle
not far from Sun Palace, our
hotel by the canal
in Naha where I sit
under chattering American helicopters
& the moon locked in a ring
of freezing mist

ready when you are
sarge

aka island (just as vast inside as out)

Beautiful to float unknowing
& snorkel with Sasha, who sings to himself
in the East China Sea
while above us, above the Kerama blue,
all is collapse
& fever check fear.

Below us:
blue devil damselfish, clownfish, stonefish, sea
snakes, sea wasps, flower urchins, jelly fish, kingdoms
of coral.

On the beach:
screwpines walk to the water
past battered patterns of flake & decay
& guardian lions & wary deer.

Joe & I march over the bridge
to Geruma Island — nothing there
but a couple of goats. Too hot
to cross the next bridge
to Fukaji, final island, where
on 26 March 1945 the 77th
Infantry Division landed
when the Americans launched their
attack against Okinawa.

At the inn:
Orion beer in the vending machine,
ludicrous crap on TV,
scuba stuff & rusty junk,
gladsome staff including
one young American guy
& his Japanese wife,
planning to stay six months.

In the town:
one bar, a restaurant
next to our inn where we eat
lunch & rent bikes to ride out
to Nishibama Beach, one tiny

grocery store, the girl
behind the counter
wearing a KISS shirt.

Forever-sound of ocean.
The smell of ants & heat.
An Aka cat sleeping
on a life jacket drying
on a wall.

Before us:
envoys from the Chinese emperor,
struggles with idiots, waves
of pleasure & relax, the sea
chewing on the shore, birdsong haze,
flame-throwers, moon
& stars sending down
light.

After us:
every breaking wave, doors opening
onto island dark,
the blue ripple-lap
at the tetrapods
tumbled at the edge,
& all that's deeper, deeper,
out there beyond.

little kids with hearing aids

have always had a peculiar power
to make me sad. More than
other obvious problems, I mean.
This may or may not be connected
to a Disney film about deaf kids
I saw at the Polson Theatre in 1981;
I could be wrong but I think
it was called *Amy*. A kid got hit
by a train & I cried in the dark.
The power to make me unhappy:
blameless little shells
on the sides of springtime heads
plugged right in the centre with
fancy technology that belongs —
clearly—in older, grizzlier ears.
Take them out or turn
them off—however they
work—& no beach waves, bird
song, Beethoven, Beatles. No Beatles!
I look at my sons, young &
smooth & mostly blameless,
& I revere their ears, which take
everything in. But maybe I'm wrong
about all this, too—if my boys could
turn the world down they'd lose
not only Nilsson & Nirvana
but also the noise of the dog next door,
kitchen arguments about money,
the diabolic squawk of Trump on tv,
my querulous bullshit about work
& weather, decrepit men sucking their teeth
& the clocks, the clocks ticking,
the clocks also blameless & busy,
lifting partitions & waving hello
& goodbye.

joe & sasha's stuff

there's something about
Joe & Sasha's stuff
lying around
when I get home
from work & they're asleep

Legos
Luke & Boba Fett
Uno cards
dinosaur robots
library books
Joe's pages of writing practice
Sasha's current temporary private interest object

(once some cucumber slices & watermelon in a bowl in the fridge
that inexplicably made me mournful)

not sure what it is
something about
their secret lives
they're alive & at play
then called away
to bath or bed

their days & business,
the evidence thereof

the flow of events
the density of their enterprise

(me tired, half-drunk maybe, standing downstairs sad)

alive all day while I'm
away

joe & sasha in the pool

    at Eight Plum Park,
    Joe's red cap & Sasha's orange one
    moving through the blue of the pool.
    Cicada chatter
    after the cloudburst.

    One other kid in the water, much younger,
    holding two plastic bullet trains. His mother,
    the older guy tending the pool, & me.

    They jump out, my sons, goggle'd, dripping,
    for sips of the milk tea I bought them
    from the vending machine down the street
    with money I got yesterday,
    payday.

    "Dada, fun!" says Sasha, & Joe
    makes the funny little yip he does sometimes
    when he's in a particularly gleeful mood.

    Last week of summer vacation. Last
    day for the pool. All the cicadas
    will be dead soon, dried out & brittle,
    & I'm grumpy because Joe
    just splashed my notebook. Day two
    without a drink.

gifu (just as vast inside as out)

    Approaching half-century on aged planet in ageless space I slide
open my door & step out into everything
there is. My house is shabby but I don't
give a shit about that—the street
is shabby—universe is shabby—
my kids & wife & I laugh & squabble-fuss
through our shabby house & la la how the life
goes on, Joe pyjama'd in the kitchen talking
to Maho, Sasha still asleep upstairs in a swastika-shaped sprawl. Meanwhile
Gifu my city all around—lived here twenty
years—considered backwater, inaka-kusai,
stinks like the country—half a million people
against old Vernon's forty thousand—& today's garbage
day: yellow mesh over the neighbourhood
pile, protection against
the neighbourhood crows. Turn
two corners to Keyaki-dori, Elm Street,
tunneled-elm gorgeous
in violent-green summer, rattle-scratch all winter—turn
left to Yanagase red light district & downtown past the Asahi
Business Hotel & porno movie house,
seamy posters with topless cops, steaming
wives, cornball sleaze, never been
in there, should go someday.
Left & right alleyways of murk & slump,
side street restaurants, a *yakuza* castle,
the boarded-up love hotel Andrij & I tried to break
into one day but couldn't & so broke
into a boarded-up hospital instead. Coming now a charm
of drunken hostesses wobbling like new-born wildebeests
on hungover heels home, little groups
of 2 or 3 with floppy cigarette hands
& there the man I see most mornings
softly walking his disabled grandson to school,
holding hands past flunk Filipina cabarets & hostess clubs with names
like *Club Memory Night* & *Club Juicy*.
My ears full of White Album Beatles, REM, Tom Waits, Leonard
Cohen, eyes full of the world & the world
behind the world, old maps, dead skin, old kisses, old romps
in love hotels, twenty years life overlaid
over everything. Trains leaving from Meitetsu Station going everywhere,

I ride three stops to Ginan work 8 hours come
back again & back through down
Tamamiya Street—the Bier Hall—my Bier Hall history—
been lovely-drunk in there with brother father sister
old girlfriends from Vernon visiting & Gifu
girlfriends before I got married—ran up
biggest tab in town, 250 000 yen worth of Bombay Sapphire
& fearless beer—cut in now for quick-shot hi
& see if my dad's business card is still tacked to the board.
At the corner meat shop stands the butcher,
his hair & beard wispy over trays of
bright red meat: hock, shank, sirloin, thin rib, silverside.
All the times I've walked this street alone
or carrying Joe or Sasha or companionable with Tom or Patrick or Max,
every step freighted with its cargo of touch & talk & time.
In the typhoon light crows on the roof of the house
where my wife grew up.
Yanagase touts rolling in now, rolling up,
the hotdog guy, the guy with one eye, the taxi drivers
& a Yanagase cat in the window
of the flower shop. Back down Keyaki-dori
past the volunteer fire station & Joe's school
with the signs all around: *Let's be kind to the flowers* & *Please take your dog shit home*. Look around, look around—look up—all the crows at dusk
dark-flying over my city as I slide
open my door & step back into
all that there is.

osho

Joe & Sasha & I walk to
Gyouza no Osho,
our fave rave restaurant.
"King of Dumplings."

Staff shouts, general
customer clamour, cooks splashing
ramen noodle water
on the kitchen's concrete floor.

Maho used to come here
with her family when she was a kid.
Chinese chow & fast & cheap.
Maho at work, now, cutting hair.

Rain & then boom & smash,
lightning & thunder. *Kaminari*
in Japanese. *Goro goro* the
onomatopoeic sound.

Whoah! people yell, rattled in their
ribcages by proximate strikes. Sasha
does an impression of a startled
kid at a neighbouring table: *Goro goro!*

Sky-hiss, & a panic of light.
Thousands killed worldwide by
lightning every year. That picture
I saw of lightning storms on Jupiter.

Our house is ten minutes away
but things are breaking up out there.
And *shit*: I left
all the upstairs windows open.

Joe points out how the neon Osho
sign turns the rain red.
We stand outside waiting for
Maho to rescue us in the car.

Sasha does an impression with his hands

of the rain on the road,
pattering his fingers down like he's playing
a tiny invisible piano.

Twenty-four years ago I sat
in my Oharu-cho doorway, 24 years old,
watching the sky-violence &
purple lightning over Nagoya.

Newly arrived & pleasantly
homesick, pleasantly sad,
missing Kia, missing Molly,
missing Stan.

Those early days: half doldrum,
half dazzle. Earthquakes poised
in the ground, typhoons curling
the air. Things preparing to happen.

Maho, growing up in Gifu,
hiding in my future. Joe
& Sasha, our fated conglomerates,
hiding in the sky.

chaotic & lovely

my son Joe
eight almost nine
sleeps like me

bigheaded longlimbed
on his back
hands on buddha belly

too tired
after swimming
at the pool

the book
he picked
open by the pillow

I have all the usual
fatherly concerns
the familiar terrors

earwig cancer
car crash earthquake
fistfight drowning

Joe's round white face
freckles, a few
& chlorine hair

generous
at all times
with his energies

likes what his body
can do
leaving no traces

his ashes
never becoming
firewood

boxing with joe

Joe joined my boxing gym when he started third grade so I pick him up after work and we bike over, companionable, Joe chatterboxing the whole way and throughout each session, *Dada, Dada*, his lungs propelling his eight-year-old voice, small and curious, into the ambient soundscape that includes whirring jump rope thwacks, heavy bag big-fist thuds, the rubbery rattling smack of the speed bag, the high insistent start and stop of the three minute timer, general shufflings and cracks and grunts, somebody yelling with every punch, somebody's ragged panting breathing, my own. And because the owner puts it on when Joe and I arrive there's also the Beatles radio channel: *I'm So Tired, Getting Better,* Joe singing along to *Strawberry Fields Forever.*

Usually: warm-up stretches, jump rope, shadow boxing, mitt practice with a trainer, heavy bag, weights, that roller wheel thingamabob, cool-down stretches. Sixty to ninety minutes.

Joe uses a stool so he can reach the speed bag. I can hear his faltering, patient practice over the sounds of Ruito and Nozomu crashing damage on each other in the ring.

When you're finished with heavy bag work you mop up your sweat with one of the yellow mops provided for that purpose. It's customary to mop up everybody's sweat, whether they're finished or not, when you mop up your own. Joe sometimes forgets this.

My mother had asthma, and recently I've felt a tightening in my chest. Try and remember to relax with the breath. Leave the breath alone.

Imagining various enemies and rivals, real and imagined, from my near and distant pasts as I belabour the heavy bag. Joe has his enemies too: mockers on the dodgeball field, unkind classmates, the fifth-grade kid who kicked him in the balls.

Jogging with my father, a long time ago. Legs and lungs working. Up and around the park and the Peanut Pool. Proud to keep up with him.

Boxing is getting back to your body, staying in the body. Boxing is getting lost in your body for three minutes at a time. Boxing is running your breath down your shoulder to your fist. I forget this sometimes.

The world is full of things that will hurt my son. Leave the things alone.

The ring floor is blue, the ring ropes red, white, and blue. The neutral corners feature a smiling cartoon tiger face with the words CHINA FOOD above and SAN COCK below. Joe and I drape our hand towels over the red top rope and do two rounds of light sparring. Very light. But if he gets lazy or sloppy I'll tap him on the forehead or belly. He needs to know.

Joe and I ride home through the summer owl light, talking. *Dada, Dada* says Joe. My breath and my heart. *Dada, Dada*. Japanese uses one character for both *breath* and *son*.

fire at midday

My mother dead 16 years today.
Stan dead almost 8 years, I think.
My wife & sons, alive in our house.
Sasha on tiptoes, doing stuff at the sink.

Yanagase policeman wiping the windows
of the police box with a rag on a pole.
Having finished his rice, my darling Joe
goes to the kitchen & washes his bowl.

Spider web in the cleavage of the statue
of Rebecca at the Well on Elm Street.
The coolness of the clouds covering the castle.
Maho outside, hanging up sheets.

A spatter of cats in Eight Plum Park,
the river running high, running low.
Still learning to dance with my sadness & panic.
First the shadow, then the crow.

little bit die

There must've been   many more   tons more
but the only scene I remember now   Stan
with the two of us listening
to The Beatles together   is from 1996   Kelowna
when we drove in your car to whatever shop   probably A&B Sound
bought *Anthology 3* on cassette   immediately
played it   driving around   making our little comments
& when McCartney's *Junk* came on
you said   'I'll say'
We were both down on McCartney in those days   weren't we, man

I also remember watching   *A Hard Day's Night*   & *Help!*
in your living room   laughing hard   all those years ago

George Harrison's dead   George Martin too
Lennon dead almost 40 years
That cruel joke: *The Beatles are dying*
in the wrong order

You dead years & years Stan   all the noise cancelled forever   can you
believe it?   Does it seem real to you?

I read somewhere that newborns need monochromatic visual stimulation
more the better   so the day after Joe was born
I took a pack of Beatle cards to the hospital   showed him, said
'These are Beatle boots'   Joe tiny frowning quiet
at all my personal Beatles ranked behind me   behind everyone

videos of Joe at 2 singing   *Love Me Do*
Sasha wide-eyed baby listening   in background crib

years later they both misheard *Live and Let Die* as   *Little Bit Die*
won't call it anything else now

downtown with Joe & Sasha last spring   we saw a baby's sock
on the road   'What's that?' asked Sasha   pointing
'Some baby's sock' I said   & Joe to the tune
of *Ticket to Ride*   sang   'Some babies don't care'

2 days ago I took Joe to Nagoya
to see McCartney   Joe's first rock show   my second Beatle

the vast steamy living room of the dome   Paul way out there
Hoffner'd   opening with *A Hard Day's Night*
singing *Something* for George   singing *Here Today* for John
singing

me crying   a little   my personal Beatles & ghosts
my life   all the rooms & scenes I've been in
beds   cars   arms   movies
& Joe   who's still so young
trying to sleep   in the middle
of the noise

in ghostly japan

    Stan your ghost of Guangzhou come to see me in Japan
        short time only summer 2000
    Your ghost is the closest we'll get
    Your ghost is the happiest I've seen it
        flashing Mao lighter patriotic commie songs
            excited in Bier Hall talking
                Things Have Changed late & drunk
                on the floor with me
    Your ghost skinny at Golden Pavilion
        funny at Meiji Mura making my girlfriend laugh
    Your ghost is full of shit Stan
        wary hungover
            ah we'll get through it &
                plunge in for more hey man?
    Your ghost is poised to triumph now
        but biofeedback bad stuff blaring
            carrying the seed of dead too soon
    Your ghost is here so lightly
        Stan what'll I do when you are far away & I am blue what'll I do
    Your ghost my friend is the stuttering engine of my foolish guilt
        I didn't go & see you in Guangzhou when I had the chance I'm sorry
    Your ghost is the only Stan there is now
    Your ghost is the photo of you I buried beside
        the Jewel Stream on Koya-san
    Your ghost Stan
        is not even past

one hour to the hereafter's deepest music

Have they eaten up all the music? All my projections: loaded with disaster. Was there music at the end of my world? A hum of wind in the elms, clatter of bamboo in the hills. We're in the future. Mother, friend, sons. Is it densely compacted? Unfold the moment & see. And hear. Tell me: have the atomic trumpets blown the trees all down. Are the orchards still tuning up?

I'm with you. We're always barely only hanging on. Canadian cities grinding in the grooves. My sons. Mother. My friend. Projected by cryptic mechanisms & stacked in the future which is not, after all, sealed out of reach. Like I thought. With you. Carried by all the old musics. Can you hear? I'm singing in your ears. I'm here.

From womb-wash to the smoking ruins to the music of Chinese panic. Is that where we are? I was there. The future's deep music, where the kids play grüch-blobs & zap doongers. Can you hear the music of the camps? Or is it the clamour of durable human joy? Which is it where we are?

Sing it to me. The music when I played your belly like a drunk. Are there Japanese sounds now? Are they icy & mountainous? Do the trees haul music out of the wind. This is the sound of me turning to reach you. With you. The voices are husks of smoke & ghost. Whale song in the whale roads, crow flap in the upper air.

Unfold the notes. Note the spaces in the middle. The black & the white & the end. Zimbabwean soot on a baobab piano. Flutes made of sun-baked cobras. Listen. I'm with you. Sailors or slaves rowing to the beat. The music. The song, & another. Can I stop? Did it? Did you hear me borrow freely?

I'm with you. Eat the music & tell me. I was there. And you.

gifu chant
    after Eduardo Galeano

Our new house made of summer.
Our new house made of riverrun bridge.
Our new house made of rhino beetles.
Our new house made of earthquake & pearl.
Our new house. We are here.

I walk my city with writing brush & knife.
I walk my city with aureate shoes.
I walk my city in elegant confusion.
I walk my city unrighteous & ludic.
I walk my city. I am here.

The air is full of Japanese bats.
The air is full of sweet potato steam.
The air is full of the sound of the mountain.
The air is full of incense, flowing.
The air is full. We are here.

The door is propped open with a big bag of rice.
The door is propped open with guardian lions.
The door is propped open with bell crickets, singing.
The door is propped open with rutilant light.
The door is propped open. You are here.

I am full of love for our new house in summer.
I am full of love for abundant walking.
I am full of love for all the air is full of.
I am full of love for the open door.
I am full of love. I am here.

acknowledgments

Poems from this collection have appeared, sometimes in slightly different versions, in *Panoply*, *Words & Whispers*, *Ulalume Lighthouse*, *Prometheus Dreaming*, *Book of Matches*, *The Closed Eye Open*, *Spectra Poets*, *Lucky Jefferson*, *Soliloquies Anthology*, *Beyond Words*, *Burnt Pine*, *The Watershed Review*, *Sheila-Na-Gig*, *Cleaver*, *New Note Poetry*, *ballast*, and *mutiny!*

Many thanks to my classmates at UBC for their intelligence & generosity & the many ways they improved these poems.

Poetical thanks to John Lent, Tom Wayman, Craig McLuckie, Sarah Tsiang, Susan Musgrave, & Bronwen Tate.

Gratitude & love to Maho, Joe, Sasha, Bumpa, Curtis & gang, Alison & gang, Noriko, Tatsuya, Dai, Hisako, Saki, David White, Stephen McKenna, & Dave Antich.

Affectionate tips of the hat to Victoria Taylor, Natasha Kachan, Erin McGregor, Kimberley Orton, Geoff Newton, Lee Shedden, Rob Kelly, & Lea Graham.

Cheers to Wayne Emde for the author-&-sons photograph.

Thank you to Michael Whone for believing in this project and being such a simpatico cat to work with.

Other Books From Bolero Bird

Lo-Fi - Michael Whone (2022)

Poor, Pretty Creature - Ciara Selene (2020)

River Van Style Review vol. 1: Gross Restore (2019)

There Is A Light That Never Goes Out - Michael Whone (2018)

Winter Lyric - Michael Whone (2017)

www.ingramcontent.com/pod-product-compliance
Lightning Source LLC
Chambersburg PA
CBHW042129100526
44587CB00026B/4230